ISBN:1983780812
ISBN-13: 978-1983780813

DEDICATION

You! This is dedicated to you! If you are reading this, it is because you are
hoping to heal yourself or a loved one, and for that I applaud you!
I hope that this book finds your soul, and provides relief.

The only people who change the world, are the ones who believe they can.

CONTENTS

The most beautiful people I have known are those who have known defeat, known suffering, known struggle, known loss, and have found their way out of the depths. These persons have an appreciation, a sensitivity, and an understanding of life that fills them with compassion, gentleness, and a deep loving concern. Beautiful people do not just happen.

- Dr. Elisabeth Kübler-Ross

PROLOGUE

Compassion is empathy free from bias;
Passion is bias free from empathy.

Over the years I've sort of developed the sense that I'm wired differently from most people. I see things differently, I experience things differently, I understand things differently, and I reflect on things differently from most people. I am backed by an almost unbridled passion and enthusiasm. I seldom "do nothing"; the concept simply doesn't exist in my vocabulary. Even now. Sometimes I feel as though I'm bordering on genius, other times I feel as though I'm bordering on crazy. And really I don't care where I am on the spectrum, or how many times the needle bounces back and forth, so long as I am rocketing forward going Mach 2 with my hair on fire. There is a lot to experience in the world, and in my lifetime, I try to bite into all of it. This has provided me a not only a high level of education, but also some life experience and wisdom. Now if this sounds conceited, I can assure you that it is not the intent. I feel as though I have something important to contribute, and as of yet, I have not found to right vehicle to contribute it. This is simply the most honest answer I have to the question "Why are you writing this?".

Having twice recovered from cancer, I am frequently approached by friends or family members, or even strangers, to give advice to a third person that has recently been diagnosed. And every time I am approached, I try to help. I believe that it's an honor, a privilege and a duty to do so. Word spread, I guess, and over time, this has actually evolved into people who are hurting, for any reason, reaching out to me for solace. But something always bothered me about giving advice to others who are hurting, and it is this. The breadth and the depth of advice I could give was limited by the amount of time I could spend with that person, by my energy and focus on that given day, and by the rate at which that person could absorb the information I was providing. Then the penny dropped, with a thundering clang. "I should simply write it out". I could summarize the cancer experiences I have had, and encapsulate the checkpoints I passed on my path to recovery. And then include the advice that I would normally give. That way everyone would receive the same product, and they would be able to absorb the material at whatever rate they wish.

I truly hope that these pages help you find the answers that you seek.

THE BARTLETT-PICKARD-SOPRANO CONNECTION

Captain of industry. Long as I can remember, I wanted to be a captain of industry. Growing up, some of my friends aspired to be professional hockey players, while others wanted to be rock stars. Now while I was once a decent hockey player, and I once played in a descent rock band, neither felt like something I fancied doing as an adult. I imagined doing something entirely different from the other kids, something I didn't even understand, except to say that is was something else. Something…Bigger.

I seem to have rushed through most of my life. I powered through honors high school and through honors post-secondary. I powered through building a solid career, while at the same time powering through rebuilding my first house. And soon, predictably, I was living beyond my means, and powering up the corporate ladder quickly in order to pay for them. I wanted a dog. I wanted a half-ton in the driveway. I wanted toys. Not to impress anyone necessarily, but because I saw them as obligatory means to an end, and the end was something…Bigger.

So what was I after? Simply put, I wanted to be a leader of men. Get married? Later if ever. Kids? Eventually. But those touchstones were far so far down on my list of priorities that I didn't even see them. As a teenager, I was fired from my first two jobs, but as the jobs I was seeking were becoming more serious, so too was my focus and attention in achieving serious results. And results came swiftly. I worked very, very, very hard. I really did, and by my mid-30s, I was on the executive fast-track. Along the way, I also (somehow) managed to meet and marry the greatest human being on the planet, and together we had the most beautiful daughter. But lucky as I was, I was going way too fast to appreciate either one of them. I was a full-blown workaholic, and I was perfectly fine with it. Achievement was paramount; all else was understood as a means to my goal.

PARDON ME SIR, CAN YOU SPARE SOME SKIN?

One day, I woke up itchy … At first it was a sort of occasional nuisance, then it became a persistent nuisance, and then finally a debilitating nuisance. A scary, bone-chilling, hair-on-the-back-of-your-neck, goose-pimpled, skin-tingling, squirming, spiders-crawling-up-your-spine, scratching-with-forks-and-knives-until-you-bleed, nuisance. Eventually I broke down and went to see a doctor, then another, and another, and another, and every one of them wanted to throw a prescription at me and say "try that". Some just told me that I was imagining it. Eventually a brilliant neurologist figured it out in about five minutes, having asked me maybe five questions. He put his hand on my knee and said "I think you have lymphoma. Probably Hodgkin's. Go get checked out immediately".

Now, you may be thinking about about how devastated I must have been in hearing that news. Truth is, I was relieved. Finally, I was validated. I wasn't going crazy. Something was just going horribly wrong inside me. Little did I know at the time, but that day would become the end of my beginning. And from that day forward, my life would take on a completely different path, with a completely different mindset. A mindset that has stayed with me to this day. A Force of some kind, be it natural force, or a spiritual force, I'll never really know, but "something" reached out and shook up the Etch-a-Sketch I had taken years, even decades crafting. What's more, that same force had to intercede not once, but TWICE. Why? Because I powered through my first cancer diagnosis and chemo the same way I powered through everything else in my life; point A to point B as fast as fucking possible, and then let me get back to work. And everything seemed to work out. Everything seemed to be back on track. The chemo was working, I was in remission, and while it was a miserable six months, I was looking forward to getting back to work. I really thought I was cured. I thought of cancer as a modest speed bump on my otherwise upward trajectory.

I got to enjoy that feeling for exactly three months.

THE BLACK PHONE & THE EYE OF THE TIGER

"If you know the enemy and know yourself, you need not fear the result of a hundred battles. If you know yourself but not the enemy, for every victory gained you will also suffer a defeat. If you know neither the enemy nor yourself, you will succumb in every battle."
— Sun Tzu, The Art of War

When you have cancer, you are subjected to all kinds of nonsense. One of which is a contrast scan. This is where the technicians inject you with a contrast dye, and then scan you for any abnormalities. In the course of my treatment these scans had become commonplace, and so I didn't think much of this one. I knew that I was feeling weird, but I had just finished six months of chemo, and figured my body was simply trying to adjust to its new normal. After all, I had been told I was cured, and so this scan was seen as confirmation that all was well.

When I went to my doctor a few days later for the scan results, my wife wanted to come along, if nothing else just to keep me company in the waiting room. So we get into the doctor's office, the doctor brings up the scan results, reads through the notes, and then does something I had never seen before or since. He says "pardon me a second". He then swings around, grabs the black phone on the wall, quickly dials a number, and begins having a conversation with someone. Still, I didn't think anything of it. I was busy thinking about what kind of taco I wanted for lunch, or something equally inconsequential. After about a minute, the doctor hangs up the phone, turns back to us and says. "Yep it's cancer. It's back". Sun Tzu was right. In my first experience with cancer, I had underestimated my opponent, I had learned nothing about myself, and so, I lost my first battle.

Now at the time I'm writing this, the reality television show Survivor is on its 30-teenth season, and I have no reason to believe the show will be ending anytime soon. People seem to love that show. It could be that it's a phenomenal show, but I simply wouldn't know. I only ever watched the first three seasons or so, and then lost interest. Those first seasons though, as a pure social experiment, what a marvelous thing those seasons were to watch. They all played out a little bit differently, but contained within each season, there seemed to be one consistent through-line. The first few episodes everybody's getting to know each other, feeling each other out, sizing each other up, and sort of moving around and toward each other.

Then around episode four, things start to get real, and slowly the contestants' facades begin to break down. At the same time, the contestants begin slowly, but gradually, chipping away at one another's facades. And then the show becomes genuinely interesting. You get to see people's true nature and motives materialize, a little bit at a time. The game itself becomes a crucible, where all irrelevancies are burned away, leaving everyone's pure product exposed. On national television.

The black phone in that doctor's office, on that day, triggered my real-life episode four of Survivor. On hearing the news, I remember turning to my wife in shock, seeing the tears and the anger start to spool up in her face, and from there I couldn't really tell you what happened. I remember going into a sort of fog driven zombie state, my ears are ringing as though I'd been shot from a canon. Whatever the doctor said after "your cancer is back", I never heard. I just kept thinking about those episodes of Survivor, and wondering, as this goes on, "what will cancer review about my true nature, and the true nature of those around me? What will my pure product look like?". I knew that no matter what, my life was about to profoundly change. Cancer was no longer inconvenient; it was about to swallow my life.

I've never been an alcoholic, but I've been around those who were, and, in hearing some of their stories, there are parallels to cancer. When an alcoholic decides to go into rehab, their friends and family generally embrace them. Relapse? The tone shifts to "get away from me". Maybe it's that people fear death, and so they start distancing themselves, or they believe that I'm putting off some sort of cancer radioactivity, where being near me afflicts you with my toxin. Some people will rush to your aid, will do anything to help you, and will provide comfort. Others will tell you that they are too overcome with emotion to approach you. Some will give you the token "call me if you need anything", and some won't care, because they are simply too busy living their own lives.

Nonetheless, when shit gets real, I promise that you will not be able to predict your own support network. Your TRUE support network. In my situation, people with whom I seemingly had only a minor role in their lives, came out of the woodwork in spades. Conversely, some of my family and friends, even my closest family and friends, disappeared. Just like Survivor, little by little, everyone in my orbit started to reveal their true nature. And frankly, so was I.

Now, to those of you who have never had to deal with a loved one with cancer, or any serious illness, let me share with you something important that I have learned. And please, take a moment, and really let this soak into your subconscious. If you know someone who is hurting, whether it is the person who is sick, or someone in their orbit, 90% of what you can do to help, is showing up. That's it. That is it. You don't need to reinvent the wheel, and you don't need to try and fix anything. You just need to be there. And if you show up, I promise you, you will forever be remembered as part of the solution. In fact, I put very little energy or attention, if any, into those that walked away from me, from my wife, from us, but I put 100% of my love and energy and attention into those that showed up, and I will continue to probably forever. In other words, in times of distress, a person becomes an island, and if you choose to stand with that person, expect to have a special place in that person's heart forever. Having carried them through pain, your footprints will have forever cemented in their "sand". But if you avoid that island, and that is your choice, expect to be out in the deep blue sea for a long, long time.

THE COLLATERAL DAMAGE

My wife is the best human being on Earth. She is a better person than I am. She is the sweetest, most kindhearted soul you will ever meet. Everybody loves her, and they should, because she's wonderful. And I've abused her. My parents are also amazing. Really amazing. So are my friends. And I've abused them too. But not on purpose. I've been married for ten years now, for example, and have never so much as raised my voice to my wife. When I mention "abuse", I'm really referring to what I will call the caregiver curse; the collateral damage caused by your illness. Think things are tough for you? Well, I can confidently tell you that things are just as tough (maybe even tougher) on those around you. And in all of the chaos of illness, the caregiver curse is something that is often ignored. When a loved one is really sick, caregivers tend to drop everything in favor of helping their loved one in need. Which is admirable. And wrong.

So to those people, the caregivers, I'm talking to you now. Are you having weight problems (gained or lost)? Are you unable to sleep? Have you withdrawn from hobbies, and interests, and family, and friends? Are you feeling increasingly hopeless? Are you having scary mood swings? Are you increasingly trying to find the solution to your problems at the bottom of a bottle or pill box? Are you dealing with headaches, exhaustion, restlessness, and despair? If you answered yes, I can relate. Or at least, my family can. Over the years that I was dealing with cancer, my family went through all of the above, and even more besides. It. Is. Hard. It is emotional abuse. It's crushing. It's depressing. It's terrible. And, it's unfair. And then suddenly, because of the caregiver curse, it's overwhelming.

So how do you get through it? Simply put, you have to let go of the things you can control. You must delegate the day-to-day tasks and errands that suck up your precious energy and time. This then frees up the time and energy you need to focus on yourself, and your loved one; the things that you cannot necessarily control. And with any serious illness, there are going to be curveballs thrown at you. Through my care network, I've learned that most people are willing to help, if YOU are willing to take the step of letting them know what you need. Whether it's doing your dishes, or hiding with you under the bed, you need to reach out and ask for whatever it is that will help you through, and keep you sane. Now, none of this is easy, but it is necessary. In fact, it's critical. Despite your best intentions, you will not be able to take care of loved ones, if you can't take care of yourself first. And if you don't take care of yourself, you are headed for a very dark place.

CHLORMETHINE AND CYTARABINE:
THE PATH TO A NEW YOU!

Chlormethine. Ever heard that word? I hadn't either. Here's a hint. The chemical also goes by the name Mustargen. Still stumped? Here's the truth. Chlormethine is a nitrogen-based analogue of mustard gas, derived from chemical warfare research. Yes. Liquid mustard gas. From the war. This is a chemical which, to this day, is still restricted or banned under international weapons conventions. And for good reason. If you get anywhere near Chlormethine, you'll experience instant and permanent damage. And if you're exposed to enough of it, you die. It is non-selective, meaning it just kills everything. And just to make it even more dangerous, Chlormethine is combustible, and under extreme conditions, becomes explosive. In other words, it's really bad shit. And if Chlormethine is "David", there is one that's still worse, the full-on "Goliath". Actually it is like Goliath's whole fucking family. It is a full-on nuclear warhead. It is Cyterabine.

You know when you get a new prescription filled at the pharmacy, and the pharmacist hands you one of those information pamphlets? It will generally list the drug, what it is commonly used to treat, dosage information, and side effects. Typical stuff. Most are a page or two. Cyterabine came with a book. A book. And while most of the pages were focused on side effects, here's a brief summary. First, nearly every side effect that I remember reading ended with "resulting in death". Second, and most crucially, it is one of the only chemo drugs that can cross the blood-brain barrier. Meaning, this poison is so strong that it can find its way into your brain. Poison. In your brain. And once it's in there, all manner of hell can break loose.

Now imagine being in a room one day, with a room of doctors and nurses, and a doctor, IV in hand, says to you: "What we are going to do, is give you two different drugs; a cocktail containing Chlormethine and Cyterabine. We will stagger them out a bit, but you will be receiving both of them. Now these will suck. Between them, you can expect abject misery. It's going to feel like a million shards of red hot lava glass are running through your body killing everything it touches, because it will be. Your mouth will immediately fill with the most awful taste, and then your mouth will start to blister and disintegrate. Your face will balloon up, and your eyes will swell shut. Your muscles will spasm and your joints will feel like they're being ripped out by white-hot claws. Your skin will jump back and forth between feeling like it's on fire, and entombed in ice. Every pain sensor in your body will be shooting sparks at the same time. And then, you will feel like you have the world's worst hangover, every minute of every day (and night). How long these sensations will last we don't really know, but we know that it's going to go on for a while. Days for sure. Perhaps weeks. Maybe more. It will be torture.

The result? Well, between the two drugs, every organ in your body will suffer immediate and lasting damage. Your hearing and your vision will take a permanent hit. Your lungs will permanently harden and scar over. You will lose every hair on your body, your nails will fall out, and then you will shed your entire stomach lining. In fact, you will shed your entire digestive system, from your esophagus to your sphincter. Gone. When you puke (and you will a lot), it will feel like throwing up fire-acid. You won't get out of bed for weeks (at least), except to change your sheets, and because your sphincter is gone, we will be changing your sheets a lot. We are going to kill everything in your body, to such a microscopic level, that you will have to get every vaccination you've ever received, once again. You will need to grow a new immune system from Ground Zero, just like a newborn. And we will have to keep you in a special place, an isolation ward, for an indeterminate amount of time while your new immune system grows, because during that time, a simple cold virus will kill you. That ward room will start to feel like a fishbowl because you will have to be continually monitored. Oh, and your fertility will be gone. Forever."

Time for a sidebar. Here's another term you have probably never heard. Neupogen. Now compared to what you have just been reading about, this one's a puppy. Simply put, this chemical stimulates your bone marrow to increase production of stem cells. Harmless enough right? There are really only two downsides to this chemical. One, it is expensive to produce. I needed 10 injections of this chemical, and each injection cost $1,000. Second, the increased cell production taxes your bones. A lot. Which hurts. A lot. All 206 bones, hurting, at the same time. And because this is bone pain, even mainline heroin won't help you. This also sucked, but it was a necessary first step. By ramping up stem cell production, extra stem cells can then be harvested, and those harvested stem cells will serve as my reset button once the chemo starts to kill me. I may never get enough stem cells to even attempt the chemo, and even if I do, there's no guarantee that the harvested stem cells aren't cancerous themselves. Anyway, this was all done in advance.

Back to the doctor: "So, all goes well, we inject the chemo, and then, you start to die. Once you're almost dead, we will re-introduce the stem cells we harvested, in the hope that your body will effectively reboot itself. Will your body reboot? We don't know. Will the chemo kill all the cancer cells? We won't know. Will we be injecting you with cancerous stem cells? We don't know. So to be safe, and assuming you survive, we will then hit you with 20 rounds of radiation. Additionally, each of these procedures brings their own unique set of risks, and side effects, and you may not notice those effects until years later."

The doctor continues "Lastly, there is one big question mark hanging over this entire process. The treatment plan I've just laid out for you, has killed athletes who were in top form. You are nowhere near top form. You have just survived 6 months of chemo, are fresh off of a stem cell harvest, and have just been cleared of near-fatal meningitis (a whole other story), and there is simply no way to know how your weakened system will respond to such an aggressive treatment. The thing is, we can't wait. Your cancer is violently spreading, and if we give you more time to recover from your chemo and your harvest and your meningitis, the cancer may quickly get beyond the point where we can even attempt treatment at all. So we have to act now. Now, while this may seem like a lot of information to take in at once, we believe that this is the best course of action. Chances? 20%. Now, if this sounds like something you want to try, sign here and let's get started".

What would you do? Now really think about this for a minute. Your impulse might be to say, "Of course, I would do it in a heartbeat!", but my experience with cancer patients has been quite the opposite. Many people with much better odds, and requiring far less treatment, opted not to do any of it. Some because they believed that the chemicals would kill them anyway, others because they wanted to enjoy what's left of their life with their loved ones at home or on a trip somewhere. Maybe you've already lived a full life and don't see the point, or maybe you're afraid of people seeing you erode down to nothing; a bald and pale skeleton. Maybe you just don't feel like being tortured. In my case, my choice was simply that I had no choice. I was young, newly married with a toddler and a dog and a mortgage and a half-ton in the driveway and toys and a lot of plans I haven't paid for yet. I would die having never gotten to know my wife properly, nor having the opportunity to see my kid develop into a person of her own, and I simply could not allow that. Plus, I had the unique experience of having almost died already once, recently, and having survived that near miss, I felt better prepared to handle what would prove to be the toughest battle of my life. However, the real battle proved to be the one that I didn't even see coming.

IS THAT A FROG ON YOUR IPOD?

Now I will spare you the gory details and trauma, and simply say that the whole experience with the chemo, the stem cell transplant, and the radiation, went pretty much as the doctors described. Perhaps worse. But my wife, and my family, and my friends (those that stood with me, anyway) were tremendous, and besides, I was too stubborn to die.

Recovery was slow going, traumatic, and more curveballs would be thrown along the way. Shingles was interesting, lung rehab was tough, and to top it all off, I went back to work, full time, way too soon. In fact, I had totally ignored aspects of my recovery, in an effort to get back to "my normal life". This ended up costing me dearly.

Like so many others out there, our household lives in an Apple ecosystem, which is to say that we have a Macbook, 5 iPhones/iPods, and 3 iPads all co-existing together. And because of this, I am well versed in Apple products. Ever get a brand new iPhone? Nice right? The battery especially seems to last forever. But over time you start to notice something. You are plugging in your phone more often. And this is because of two reasons. First, 100% charge ain't what it used to be, and second, it takes longer to get there. Eventually you are charging to 80%, then 70%, then 50%, and the charges are taking longer and longer, until eventually your phone is perma-tethered to the wall. A laptop does the same.

Needless to say, my half-ass recovery followed a similar trajectory. And since I went back to work way too soon, I basically started on 60% charge. It took another two years of trying harder and harder (and taking longer and longer) to charge up my "batteries", only to find ever-shrinking energy reserves on tap. So why did I let it get to that? Why didn't I stop myself sooner? Look at it another way. Ever try throwing a frog into boiling water? Me neither, but I'm sure that if you did, the damn thing would jump out of the pot quicker than you got it in there in the first place. If you want the cook a live frog, I've learned, the trick is to place it in a pot of comfortable water, and then slowly bring the water up to boiling. That way, the frog won't jump out, and by the time it realizes that it's in trouble, it's cooked. This is precisely what happened to me. I always believed that I would get better, and that belief clouded what was really going on. Besides, my condition was worsening in such slow increments, that I didn't even notice until it was too late.

Eventually, it got so bad, that I devolved from living, to simply existing. My life slowly, but steadily, ground down to a halt. I was totally out of gas. It would take me an hour, and three cups of coffee, to summon the strength to brush my teeth (if I did at all). The volume on everything was turned way down. Everything seemed far away and surreal. Like a copy-of a copy-of a copy. And I was left tethered to maybe three rooms in my house.

Boiled. Cooked. Toast…And then it got worse.

GORDON RAMSAY'S RECOVERY RECIPE

For many years now, I have been the "Turkey-Maker" in the house, and I am actually pretty good at it. I've tried everything from brining to smoking. I even cooked one with a torch. I have made my own herb butter and rubbed it meticulously under the skin, and I have simply said "I'll have none of that" and bought a Butterball. Regardless of how you make your turkey, though, I have learned that there is one thing which you must always do. It is a trick I learned from Gordon Ramsay. Simply put, you need to let a turkey rest in equal measure with how long you allow it to cook. So a 3-hour cook is accompanied by a 3-hour rest. The only caveat is that you must keep the turkey above 140 degrees to remain food-safe. And if you do this, I promise that you will have the best turkey you can imagine. People will LOVE it.

The same can be said for cancer. In fact, the same can be said for any major life-threatening event; be it military combat, a natural disaster, a car accident, or a sexual assault. If something you witnessed or experienced affected you enough to warrant treatment, any treatment, you must allow equal time for healing. And this is important. A lot of people make the same mistake I did, and assume that if they are feeling better, then it's time to return to work. Wrong. Cancer took years to beat, and it will take years to recover. Not just physically, but emotionally. And, take it from me, if you are someone who tends to ignore your emotions, you'd better learn to face them head-on, and quick, or you will find yourself in a whole 'nother battle. The war at home. The war in your head.

And this war is far harder than anything else you ever had to endure...

"MIND IF WE COME OVER IN A FEW MINUTES?"

The fastest I ever clean my house is in the ten minutes before I know someone's on their way over. Now, my house is usually pretty clean, but I always feel compelled to spend that ten minutes putting the dishes away, or sweeping the floor, or putting the magazines and the mail away, whatever. Now imagine that you have one thing left out of place, and the doorbell rings. What do you do? I just grab that thing, chuck it in my attached garage, and tell myself that I'll deal with it later. But what about the next time? More people on their way means more stuff shoved away, until eventually you run out of hidey-holes. My garage, at one point, was my worst offence by far. A three-car garage that wouldn't fit any cars. It got so bad that I could barely close the doors to contain it.

But you keep thinking "it's fine. Out of sight, out of mind. I'll get there eventually", but someday never comes. And then suddenly, one day, it's too much. I don't remember exactly why (perhaps it was that winter was coming and my wife hates the cold), I had to clean the garage. I had to. Only this time, I attacked it differently. Not only did I clean up the clutter, I ended up pulling everything off of every shelf, out of every drawer, and out of every nook and cranny. I was left with a GIANT pile of random stuff on the garage pad. Things I had been looking for, certainly, but also things that I had forgotten all about. Frankly, there were things in there I didn't even know I had. But I knew that standing there, looking at this huge pile, I would force myself to deal with all of it. And I promised myself, that for every item on the pad, I would find an appropriate and permanent place to park it.

This, in a nutshell, is PTSD. You take emotions, thoughts, and traumas, and rather than dealing with them, you keep shoving them into your mental garage. You keep thinking "it's fine. Out of sight, out of mind. I'll get there eventually", which works up to a point, but eventually, and ultimately, winter comes or the garage door lets go, and you are left with an explosion of things everywhere. And the only way to truly know what you are dealing with, is to take everything out and examine it. Only the things you examine are all very scary. Panic attacks. Insomnia. Crushing despair. Anxiety. Dissociative episodes. Overwhelming fatigue. Paralyzing sadness. Screaming-in-the-ears. Addictive behavior. Self-destructive behavior. Stress. Depression. Nightmares. Mania. Hallucinations. Flashbacks. Intrusive Thoughts. Uncontrolled Rage. Tears. Grief. PAIN.

Now, some of those things were things that I knew were there, and that I knew I had to confront, but there were also things that I had completely forgotten about or suppressed. Frankly, there were things in my mind that I didn't even know I was experiencing. But I knew that standing there, looking at this huge mess, I would force myself to deal with all of it. And I promised myself, that I would learn what to do and how to deal with each thing, individually. Now this takes a long, long time. In fact, it took me a year to even begin to figure it out. And my path to recovery is still being built as I walk on it. But I am building it. Everyday.

A MAN FALLS INTO A HOLE

This guy's walking down a street when he falls in a hole. The walls are so steep; he can't get out. A doctor passes by, and the guy shouts up, "Hey you, can you help me out?" The doctor writes a prescription, throws it down in the hole and moves on. Then a priest comes along, and the guy shouts up "Father, I'm down in this hole, can you help me out?" The priest writes out a prayer, throws it down in the hole and moves on. Then a friend walks by. "Hey Joe, it's me, can you help me out?" And the friend jumps in the hole. Our guy says, "Are you stupid? Now we're both down here." The friend says, "Yeah, but I've been down here before, and I know the way out." – Aaron Sorkin.

Ever been to therapy? How did you feel about it? Personally, until I was diagnosed, I thought that therapy was for pussies. And when I began therapy, at my doctor's urging, I went in with that very pre-conceived notion. I didn't want to talk about my feelings, in fact, I didn't want to talk at all. I was closed off at best, and combative at worst. Ever quit smoking or lost weight? How did you do it? I guarantee that you did not succeed because someone else told you that you needed to. You succeeded because you convinced yourself that you could, and simply…began. Maybe you started cutting back on your bad habits. Maybe you chewed gum or took pills. Maybe you joined a gym. Regardless, you did one crucially important thing; you opened yourself up to the prospect of change, and tapped into a kind of inner strength. And I'll bet you surprised yourself with what you were able to accomplish, once you committed to doing the work…

Back to our guy in the hole. If you are hurting, emotionally, and if you think that it will just get better, you are kidding yourself. Seriously. If you think therapy alone, or medication alone, or prayer alone, will make you better, you are also kidding yourself. What you need to do is ALL of it. You have to convince yourself that you can do it, that you can heal, and then, you have to commit to doing the work. But I'll add one more. You need to talk to someone like you. For me, since I didn't know anyone with PTSD, this meant going to group therapy. And once I opened myself up to it, it became the silver bullet for my recovery. And I found my inner strength. Sometimes I was being carried by someone, other times I was the one doing the carrying. But as a group, we held each other up, and together, we each found our way out of our hole. And #FiveMinutes was my way out…

AFTER THE MUD, THE BLOOD & THE BEER…

Honestly, looking back, I feel like I should be angrier at everything I have endured. I should be angrier at years of my marriage lost to Jayne playing the role of caregiver, or at the times I helplessly spent watching someone else play with my daughter, walk the dog, or spend time at the cabin. I should be angrier at being, for the first time, that kid that watches with longing all of the other kids play outside, from inside his bedroom window. I should be angrier at the thought that countless years have been taken from me due to the chemo.

The truth is, I am not. The way I see it, I was dealt a bum deal, period; and the only way to get though it is to suck it up and get through it. You can either say "this is it. This is how I end". Or you can get to work. You just…begin. I can deal with the hundreds of needles, the gallons (yes, gallons) of chemo, and the constant ringing in my ears, and the pills. And I can deal with losing a lung, the crippling pain, the countless sleepless nights, and the unending fatigue.

And I can deal with being nearly killed by cancer, and meningitis, or the countless trips to the hospital, or being the cause of so much pain to my family. And I can deal with missing my daughter's first day of preschool, or hearing her describe daddy to others as "sick" or "in the hospital". And I can deal with watching my wife cry, or trying her hardest to hold back her tears, and having nothing to say to comfort her. And I can deal with the resulting infertility. Perhaps I was meant to see that selfless kindness and charity DO still exist. Perhaps I was meant to savor life, rather than hustle through it.

In the meantime, I have already survived 100% of my worst days. I am closer to my wife than ever. I have a great relationship with my daughter. I have renewed relationships with my sister, my mom, my dad, and my in-laws. My entire network of friends and extended family have been brought in closer, and have taught us who really cares, who pretends, and who never did. Every day, I get up, and I try to clap my hands together and say: "Today's gonna be a great day". The doctors and nurses call it my "new normal". And I will endeavor to make the new version of myself stronger, more focused, and more appreciative of what I have around me; all with a renewed sense of purpose.

And my renewed purpose is this. One day, twenty years from now, my daughter will be talking to me about this era in history. Both on a personal level and on a broader, human level. And my fear is that, during that discussion, she will stop and ask "Wait a minute. You mean to tell me that you knew this was a problem, but you didn't do anything about it?". I AM doing something about it. Right now, today. I am committing myself to listening, helping, and coaching others through pain, real pain, and I will let that advocacy take me wherever it goes, for however long it goes. Maybe this is the "something bigger" that I have been searching for. Maybe this is the meaningful way that I can contribute to the greater good. Maybe this is the path I was meant to walk, all along. I am going to face the difficult issues, and I am going to put them front and center.

Now this will take courage, but I am not afraid. I will not be bullied by fear. I am going to give it everything I've got, and I'm going to leave it all out on the proverbial field. And then, I will accept the judgement of history. Success is how high you bounce when you hit the bottom, so prepare to watch me bounce, bitches. Bring. It. On.

MY CHALLENGE TO YOU! #FIVEMINUTES

Hi. It's me. Ryan. And I need you to slow down and give me five minutes of your time. This is for real.

I've learned something life-changing today. Just today! And it's this. To be soft, to expose your soft little underbelly in today's cynical world, takes...courage, and courage requires strength. It takes BALLS. It is not a weakness. And if an example is required, then I will provide one, right now. So to those of you out there who are "hurting", really hurting, and you know who you are, please reach out to me. Now this may be awkward, but seeing as I'm the first one to do it, it has to start with me and you. And if you reach out to me, I promise you five minutes of uninterrupted, no phones, no distractions, no bullshit, undivided attention, to hear your story. To listen. I won't judge, and I may not even understand, but I will listen.

Five. whole. minutes. Let's call it #FiveMinutes. If you're worried that sharing your story will make you cry, know that I already cried while writing this. There, I said it. And if, after that five minutes of uninterrupted time, you feel better; if, after that five minutes you feel RELIEF, reach out to someone else, anybody else, whether they are friends or basic strangers, but someone that you know is really hurting, and promise them five minutes of your uninterrupted time. To listen. You can probably picture that person in your head right now. It will be awkward. But if at the end of those five minutes, the person you listened to feels better, insist, insist that they reach out to someone they know who is hurting, And so on. Trust me on this: When you are hurting, the best way to heal, the best way to really heal, is to help someone through their pain. If not me, share #FiveMinutes with someone else, because that sigh of relief that your soul will give you is the first step... But talk to someone. And if you do choose me, if you are willing to expose your soft underbelly to me, I will admire your courage, and I will applaud your strength. And I will listen. And then I will ask "Where do we go from here? And how can I help you get there? What can I do?". You may respond with "I'm good", or you may say "I would like to do this again". Who knows? No matter what though, I promise to do whatever I can do to help. Now, I don't know how many people are going to take me up on my offer, but I hope it's at least one.

So, to that person out there who is hurting, I am listening...I'm in!

#FiveMinutes